Pebble® Plus

LET'S LOOK AT COUNTRIES

LET'S LOOK AT
BRAZIL

BY JOY FRISCH-SCHMOLL

raintree

a Capstone company — publishers for children

Raintree is an imprint of Capstone Global Library Limited, a company incorporated in England and Wales having its registered office at 264 Banbury Road, Oxford, OX2 7DY – Registered company number: 6695582

www.raintree.co.uk
myorders@raintree.co.uk

Edited by Erika L. Shores
Designed by Juliette Peters
Original illustrations © Capstone Global Library Limited 2020
Picture research by Jo Miller
Production by Kathy McColley
Originated by Capstone Global Library Ltd
Printed and bound in India

ISBN 978 1 4747 6940 2 (hardback)
ISBN 978 1 4747 6958 7 (paperback)

British Library Cataloguing in Publication Data
A full catalogue record for this book is available from the British Library.

Acknowledgements
Getty Images: Bambu Productions, 13, Otavio de Souza/Stringer, 15; Newscom: Sipa USA/ Gilson Borba/NurPhoto, 14; Shutterstock: Aleksandar Todorovic, 1, Alf Ribeiro, Cover Middle, Bram Smits, Cover Bottom, Cover Back, BrazilPhoto, 17, Bruno Ismael Silva Alves, 19, Erni, 9, Filipe Frazao, 11, GlobeTurner, 22 (Inset), Gustavo Frazao, 7, Kleyton Kamogawa, 22-23, 24, marchello74, 21, nate, 4, Nick Fox, 8, R.M. Nunes, 5, Skreidzeleu, 3, SNEHIT, Cover Top

Every effort has been made to contact copyright holders of material reproduced in this book. Any omissions will be rectified in subsequent printings if notice is given to the publisher.

All the internet addresses (URLs) given in this book were valid at the time of going to press. However, due to the dynamic nature of the internet, some addresses may have changed, or sites may have changed or ceased to exist since publication. While the author and publisher regret any inconvenience this may cause readers, no responsibility for any such changes can be accepted by either the author or the publisher.

CONTENTS

Where is Brazil?

Brazil is the largest country in South America. It covers almost half the continent. Brazil's capital city is Brasília.

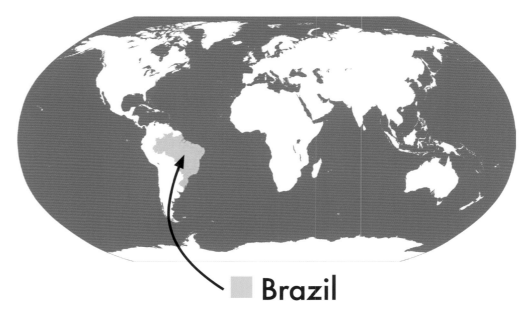

Brazil

Brasília, Brazil

From rainforests to beaches

The Amazon River and the surrounding rainforest are in Brazil. Brazil also has hills, wetlands and beaches. The weather is warm and wet all year.

The wild side

The rainforest is full of life.

Monkeys and parrots live in the trees. Huge snakes called anacondas live in rivers. Wildcats hunt capybaras.

common squirrel monkeys

capybaras

People

The first Brazilians were Amerindians.

Starting in the 1500s, people came

from Portugal. Later, more people

came from Europe and Africa.

Most Brazilians live in large cities.

At work

Half of Brazilians work in jobs

that help other people. These jobs

include doctors, dentists and teachers.

Farmers grow sugar cane and coffee.

Ranchers look after cattle.

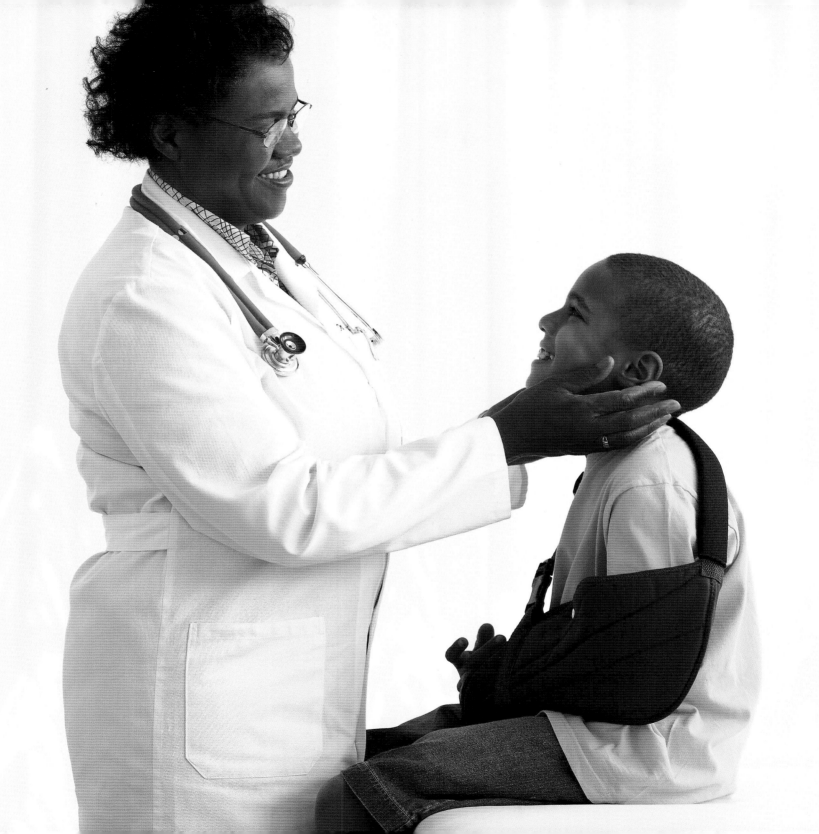

Carnival

Carnival is a festival in Brazil. It lasts one week. It happens just before Lent. People wear costumes and march in parades. They play music and dance in the streets.

Kick! Score!

Football is Brazil's main sport.

Children play it on fields and in streets.

Brazil's national team plays in
a large stadium. Brazil have
won the World Cup five times!

Time to eat

Many Brazilians eat a lot of rice and beans. One popular dish is feijoada. It has black beans and smoked meat.

19

Famous place

A tall statue overlooks the city of Rio de Janeiro. It is called Christ the Redeemer. Its open arms welcome people to Brazil.

QUICK BRAZIL FACTS

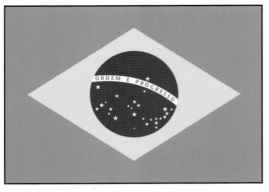
Brazil's flag

Name: Federative Republic of Brazil

Capital: Brasília

Other major cities: São Paulo, Rio de Janeiro, Salvador

Population: 207,353,391 (2017 estimate)

Size: 8,515,770 sq km (3,287,957 square miles)

Language: Portuguese

Money: Real

GLOSSARY

Amerindians Indians native to South America

anaconda very large snake found in South America

capybara large, furry rodent that does not have a tail

continent one of Earth's seven large land masses

Lent the 40 days before the Christian celebration of Easter

rainforest thick forest of green plants that receives rain all year long

wetland land that is low and wet, such as marshes or swamps

FIND OUT MORE

BOOKS

Animals in Danger in South America (Animals in Danger), Richard and Louise Spilsbury (Raintree, 2014)

Brazil (A Benjamin Blog and His Inquisitive Dog Guide), Anita Ganeri (Raintree, 2015)

Introducing South America (Introducing Continents), Anita Ganeri (Raintree, 2014)

WEBSITES

www.bbc.com/bitesize/articles/zr2h47h
Explore Rio de Janeiro!

www.dkfindout.com/uk/earth/continents/south-america
Find out more about South America.

COMPREHENSION QUESTIONS

1. Look at the photo of capybaras on page 9. Describe other animals you know of that are similar to capybaras.

2. Describe Carnival. What do you think it would be like to go to Carnival in Brazil?

3. Name one thing that farmers grow in Brazil.

INDEX